Adrian Le Roy

Fifth Book of Guitar Tablature
For Low G Ukulele

Transcribed from the

Cinqiesme Livre De Guiterre, Contenant Plusiers
Chansons a Trois & Quatre Parties, Par Bons & Excelens
Musiciens: Reduites en Tabulture par Adrian Le Roy

ISBN: 978-1-387-45561-4

Table of Contents:

CINQIESME LIVRE DE GVI-
TERRE, CONTENANT PLVSIEVRS CHANSONS A TROIS
& quatre parties, par bons & excelens Musiciens: Reduites en Tabu-
lature par Adrian le Roy.

5

TABLE.

A PARIS.

De l'imprimerie, d'Adrian le Roy, & Robert Balard, Imprimeurs du Roy, rue
saint Iean de Beauuais, à l'enseigne sainte Geneuieue.
6. Decembre.
1554.

Auec priuilege du Roy, pour neuf ans.

Short Biographies

Jacob Arcadet *(c. 1505-1568) was a Franco-Flemish composer active in Florence, Rome, and Paris. He was known for his madrigal works and produced several volumes throughout his career. He was also well known for composing chansons, especially when, in 1551, he returned to Paris from Italy where he had been appointed to the Papal choir at St. Peter's Basilica in Rome. Arcadet's chansons represent the bulk of Adrian Le Roy's Cinquiesme Livre de Guiterre published in 1554 by which time he was already in the service of Cardinal Charles de Lorraine. The appearance in Du Chemin's chansons Nouvelles of many pieces by Arcadet anticipate the growing prominence of his music.*

Laurent Bonard *was a priest and Maistre des Enfants at the Cathedral of Amiens between 1547 and 1553. Only one of Bonard's chansons was included in the Cinquiesme Livre de Guiterre but there are at least five additional chansons which were published by Du Chemin ascribed to "Bonardo" who was most likely the same composer. Bonard returned to Italy and was the author of a book of madrigals published in Venice in 1565.*

Pierre Certon *(d. 1572) was a French composer active chiefly at the Sainte Chapelle du Palais from 1532 until his death. Closely associated with the French royal court and with its official printer Attaingnant, he is credited with over three hundred chansons in the publications of Attaingnant, Du Chemin, and Le Roy and Ballard.*

De Bussy *(f.1553 – 1583) little is known of this composer except that he may have lived in Paris during the years 1553 to 1583 and contributed chansons to a good number of music books published by Le Roy and Ballard.*

Adrian Le Roy *was an accomplished musician and entered the service of, first, Claude de Clermont, then, Jacques II (Baron de Semblançay and Viscount of Tours), and both members of the aristocracy who had influence at court. In 1546, he met the publisher Jean de Brouilly in Paris and married his daughter Denise de Brouilly.*

Le Roy and his cousin Robert Ballard (ca. 1525-1588) founded the printing firm "Le Roy & Ballard", and in August 1551 obtained a royal privilege from Henry II to print music. In February 1553, the company was awarded the title of "imprimeur du Roi en musique." Over the following two decades, other rival companies dropped out of the market and from the 1570s onwards Le Roy & Ballard enjoyed a virtual monopoly in music publishing in France.

While Robert Ballard looked after the business side, Le Roy was the artistic director. He achieved renown as a composer and arranger of songs and instrumentals, his published work including at least six books of tablature for the lute, 5 volumes for the guitar and arrangements for the cittern.

Le Roy died in Paris in 1598.

The Renaissance Guitar:

The first instruments that might be recognized as true guitars were built in the fifteenth century. Renaissance guitars were believed to be much smaller than their modern counterparts, with double courses for the lower three strings and a single string, (called a quinta or chanterelle), for the highest-pitched string. This provided a rich sound and encouraged strumming the guitar to the accompaniment of singers.

The guitar also had tied gut frets, friction tuning pegs, a decorative rose, a bridge set near the bottom of the instrument, and sometimes a rounded rather than flat back. Its courses of double strings were tuned in the intervals of fourth, major third, and fourth (for example, g/g-c/c-e/e-a), often with the lowest course in octave rather than unison doubling.

The four-course guitar enjoyed a rich repertory in the sixteenth century that included dances, fantasias, chansons, and other secular genres. The instrument was widely played in France, Italy, England, and throughout Spain and Portugal. Four-string guitar repertory includes works by the Spanish composers Alonso Mudarra (ca. 1510-1580), Miguel de Fuenllana (died after 1568), and Juan Vasquez (ca. 1510-ca. 1560); the Italian composer Melchiore de Barberiis (published 1549) and lutenist Alberto da Ripa (ca. 1500-1551); the French composer Guillaume Morlaye (published 1550); and the printers Adrian Le Roy (ca. 1520-1598) and Pierre Phalèse (ca. 1510-1573).

I recommend placing a capo on either the third or fourth fret to better imitate the higher pitch of the renaissance guitar. Remember, only the highest four strings of the guitar are needed for all of the compositions here.

Understanding Tablature:

Tablature for the Renaissance guitar and the Ukulele presents the four strings of the instrument arranged from top to bottom. The four lines represent the highest four strings on the guitar - the low D is at the bottom followed by G, B, and the high E. For the ukulele, the low G is followed by C, E, and high A. Each number on a string directly indicates a fret, 1 meaning the first fret, and 10 meaning the tenth fret. A "0" would indicate that the string is played openly.

Chords are indicated by numbers appearing vertically and single notes commonly designate solo playing or chord arpeggios.

In the example that follows, the piece begins with a simple chord. The ring finger of the left hand is placed on the third fret and all four strings of the ukulele or the highest four strings of the guitar are played simultaneously.

This is followed by lifting the ring finger and allowing the middle finger to stop the highest string on the second fret and strike that string only. The string is then struck open, that is, the left hand is off the fretboard completely. The ring finger on the left hand then returns to the third fret on the highest string and that string is struck and so on.

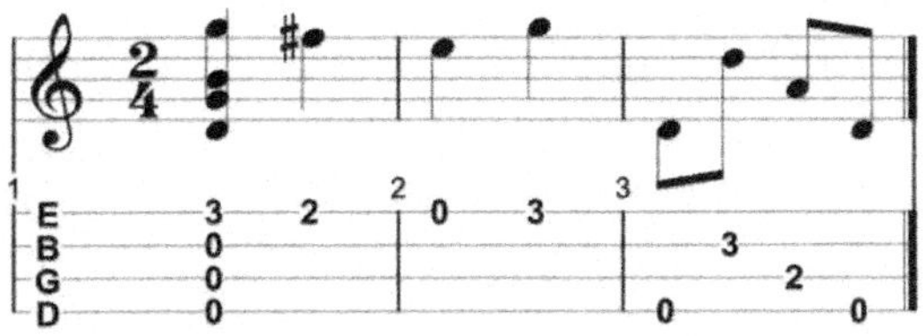

Ornamentation:

The music presented here has been transcribed exactly as it appeared in the original manuscript from 1546 and can be played exactly as written. Renaissance musicians, however, would have embellished each piece with various divisions and graces. When playing these pieces, you are invited to experiment with different ornaments and make these pieces your own.

In renaissance music, ornaments or embellishments are musical flourishes that are not necessary to carry the overall line of the melody (or harmony) but serve instead to decorate or "ornament" that line. Many ornaments are performed as "fast notes" around a central note. Further, rhythm changes might also be made. Graces might include a hammer-on or pull-off. When you see chords, consider strumming the chord, arpeggiating the chord, or adding mordents or trills.

The Music:

The compositions which follow are presented in the same order as they appear in the original work. They were transcribed from a facsimile edition of the original manuscript and every effort has been made to transcribe the original tablature accurately into modern tablature. Should you find any errors, I would be happy to make corrections in future editions. I can be contacted through this publisher.

Escoutez ma complainte

De Bussy 1553 -1583

Tablature by Michael Walker

8va
A
E
C
G

L'Esté Chault Boulloit

Adrian Le Roy - 1520-1598

Tablature by Michael Walker

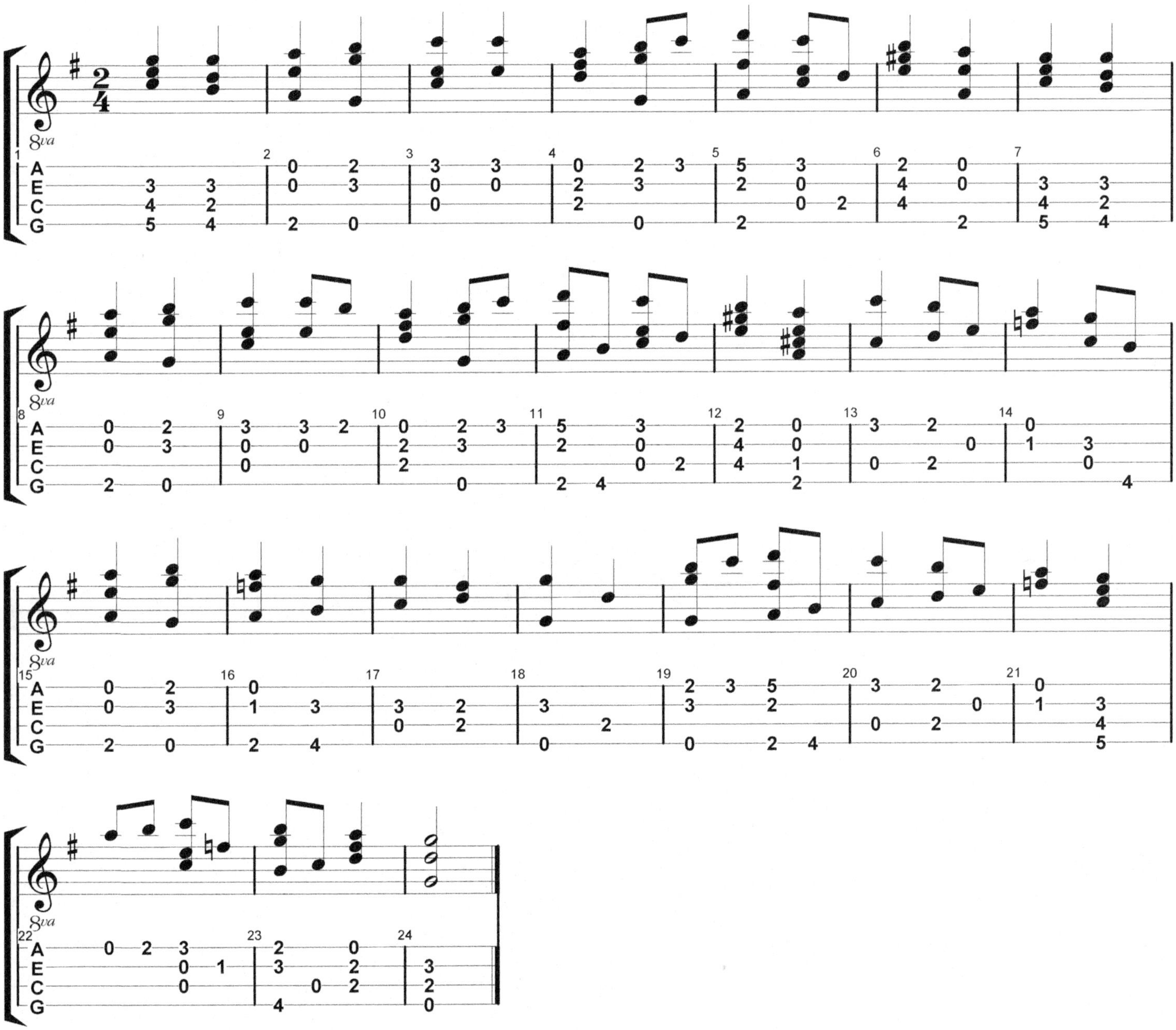

Je ne me confesseray point

Jacob Arcadet 1505 - 1568

Tablature by Michael Walker

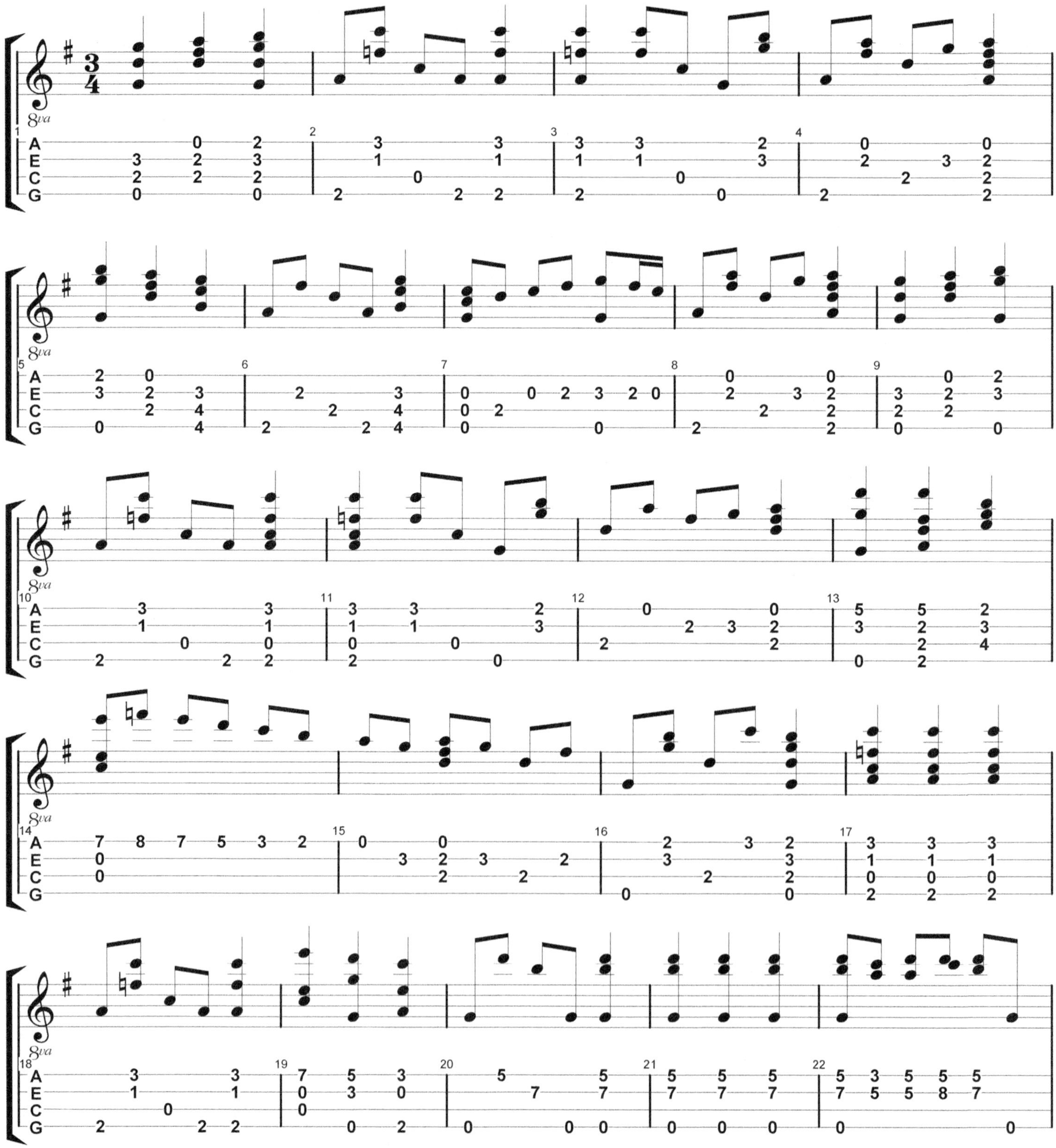

Au Jour Au Jour

Laurent Bonard 1547 -1554

Tablature by Michael Walker

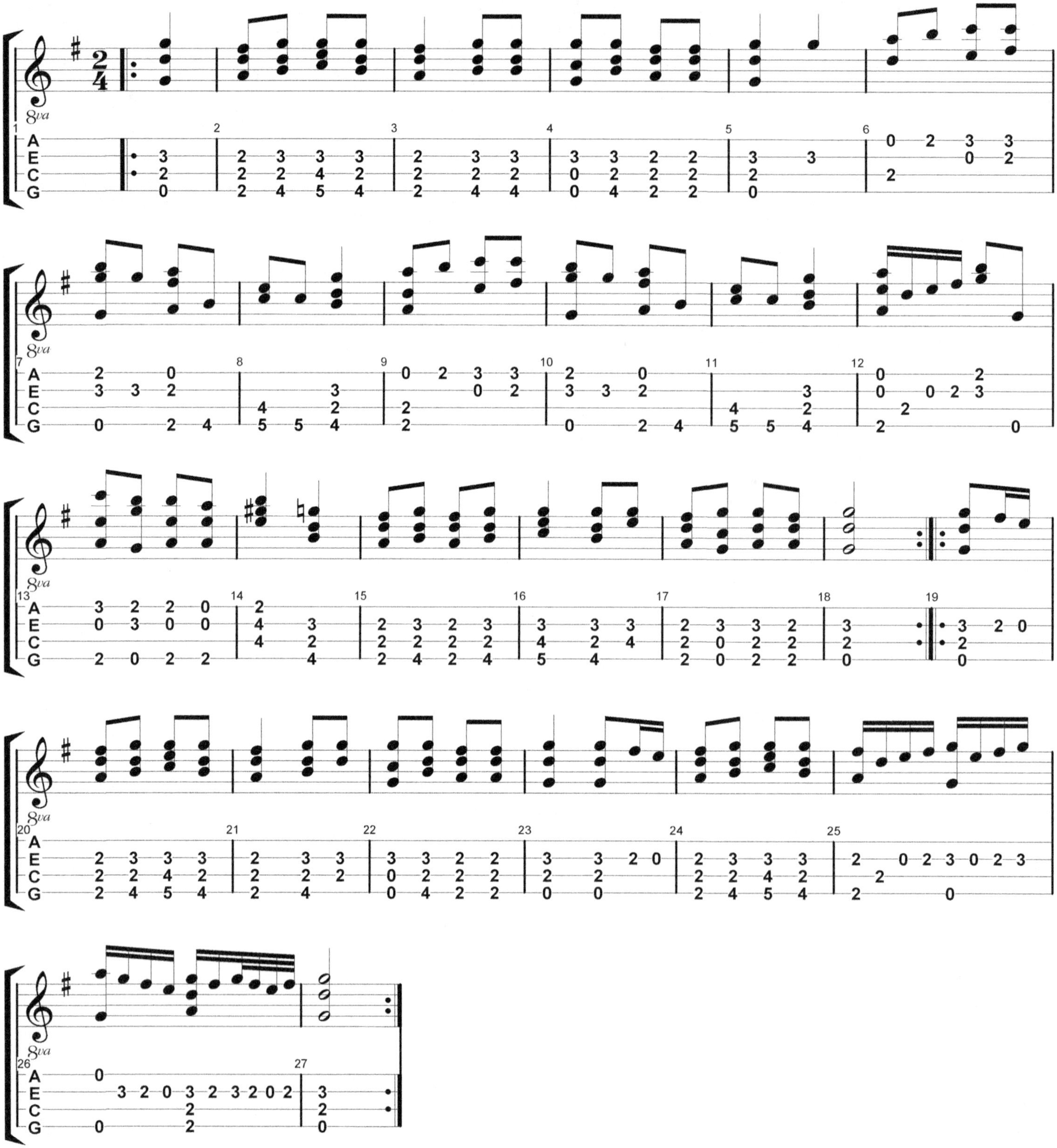

Quand Viendra La Clarte

Jacob Arcadet 1505 - 1568

Tablature by Michael Walker

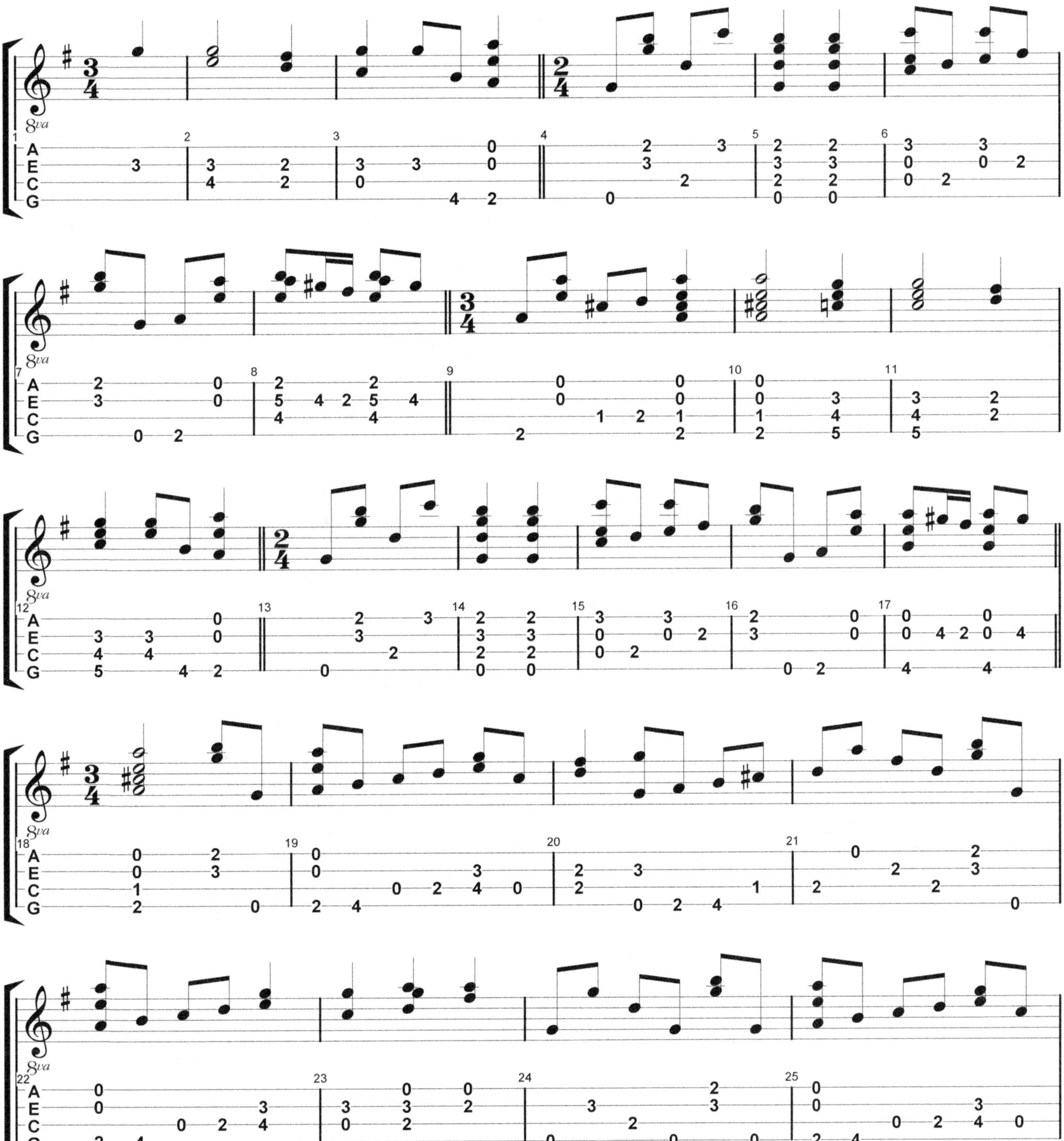

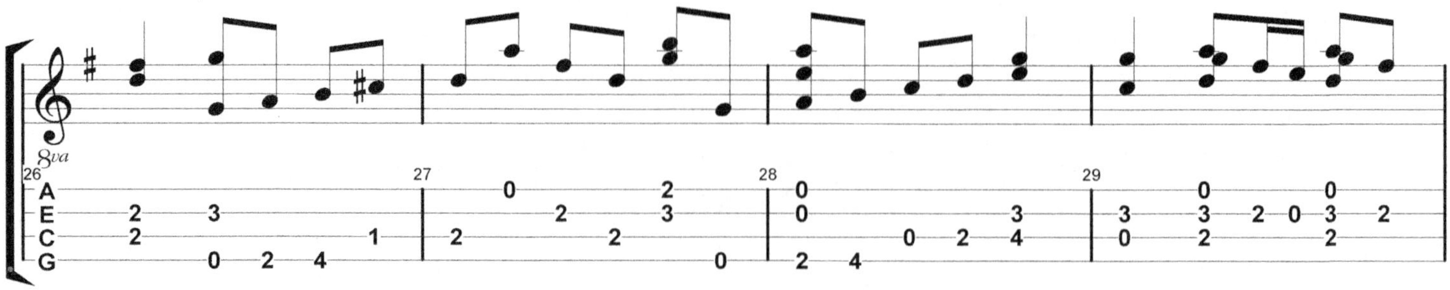
8va
26
A
E
C
G
27
28
29

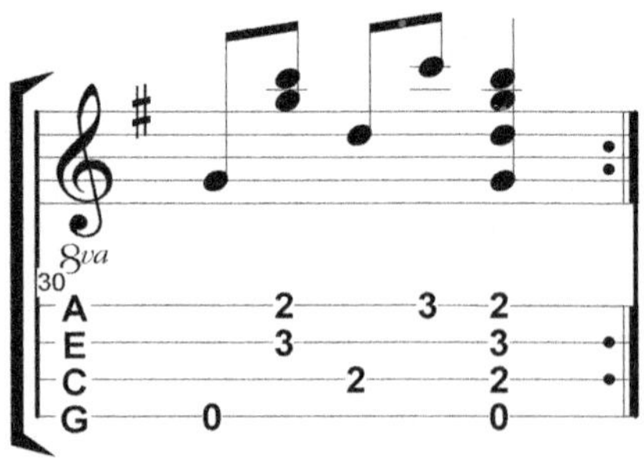
8va
30
A
E
C
G

Je Ne Scay Que C'est Quil Ma Faut

Jacob Arcadet 1505 - 1568

Tablature by Michael Walker

8va
A
E
C
G
25
26
27
28
29
30
31
32
33
34
35
36
37

Que te sert amy d'estre ainsi

Jacob Arcadet 1505 - 1568

Tablature by Michael Walker

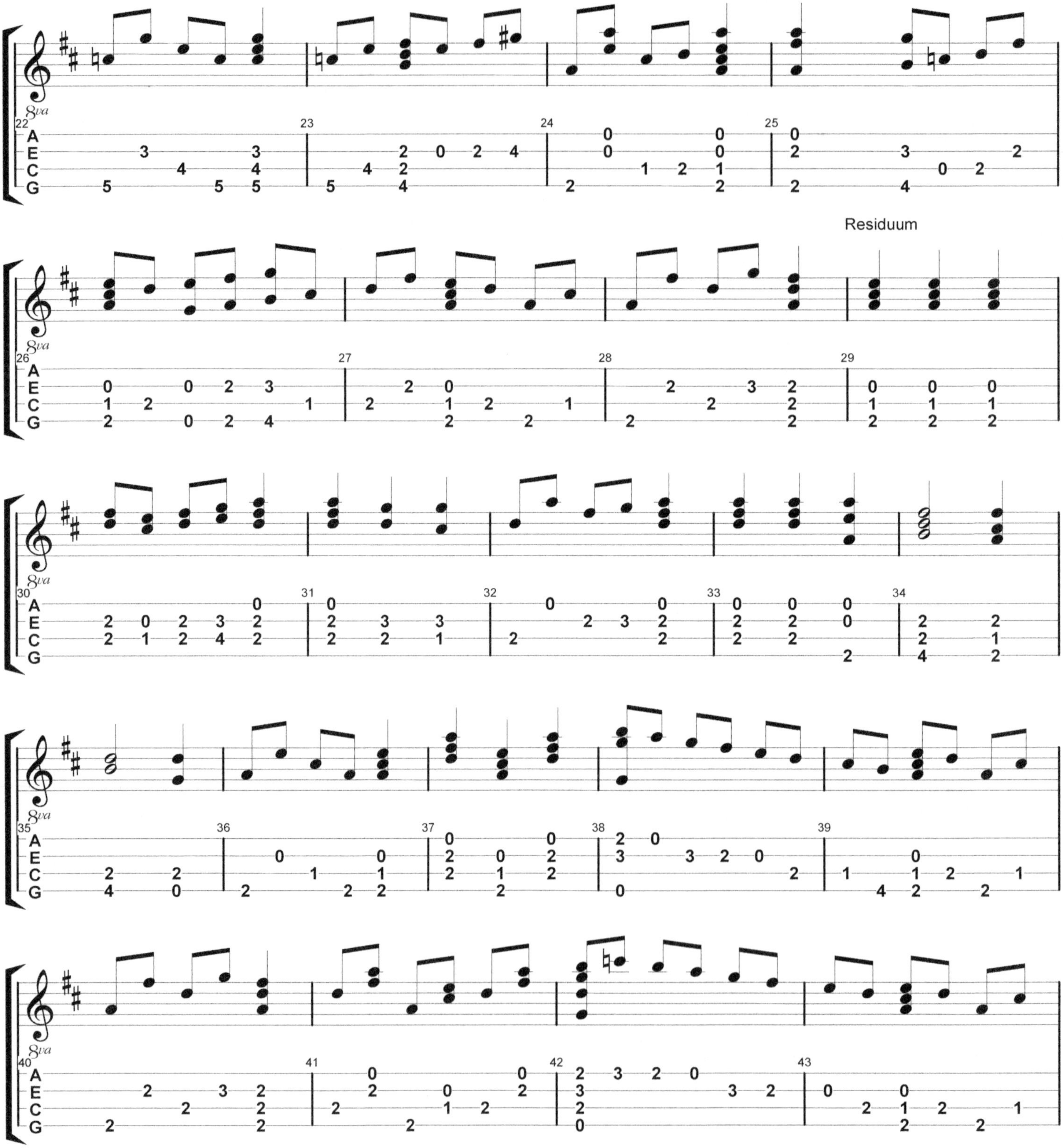
Residuum

Que te sert amy d'estre ainsi - Jacob Arcadet 1505 - 1568

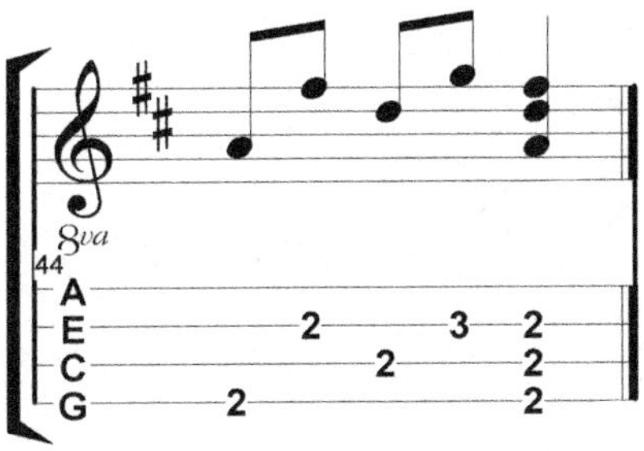

J'ay tant bon credit qu'on voudra

Jacob Arcadet - ca. 1505 - 1568

Tablature by Michael Walker

8va
A
E
C
G

Dieu Inconstant

Jacob Arcadet 1505 - 1568

Tablature by Michael Walker

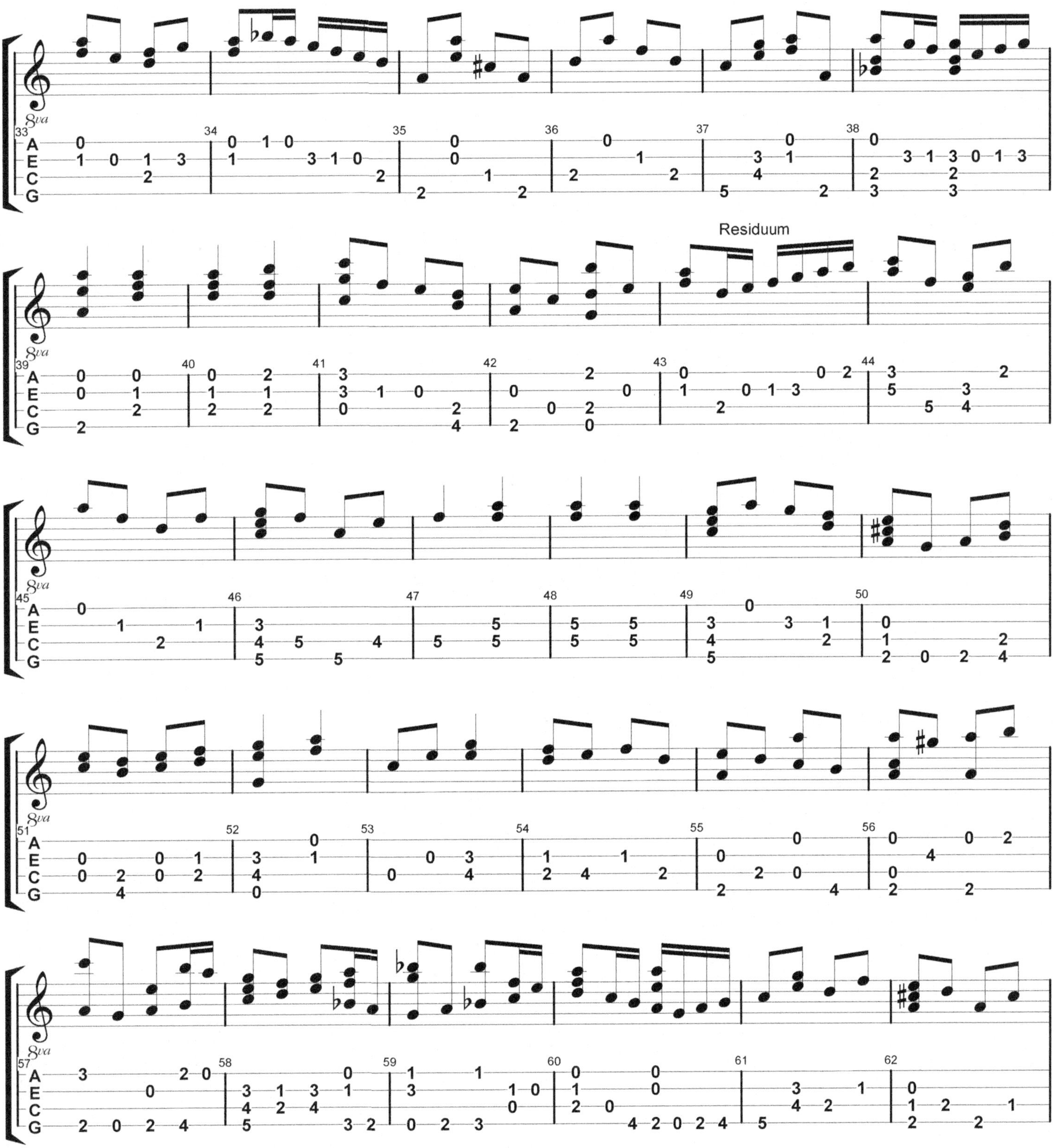
Residuum

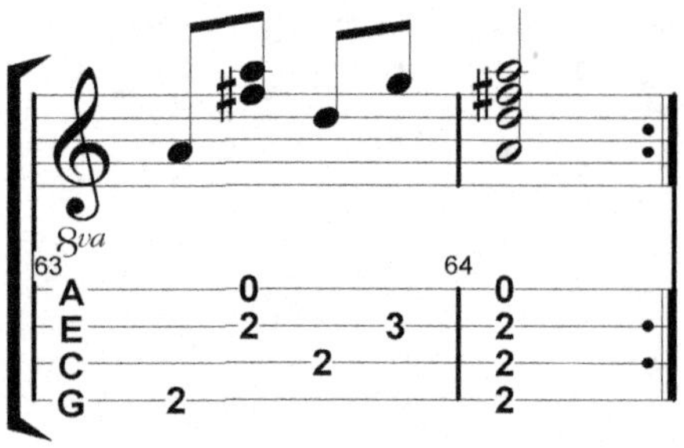
8va
63
64
A
E
C
G
0
2
3
2
2
0
2
2
2

Ce n'est bien ny plaisir

Jacob Arcadet 1505 - 1568

Tablature by Michael Walker

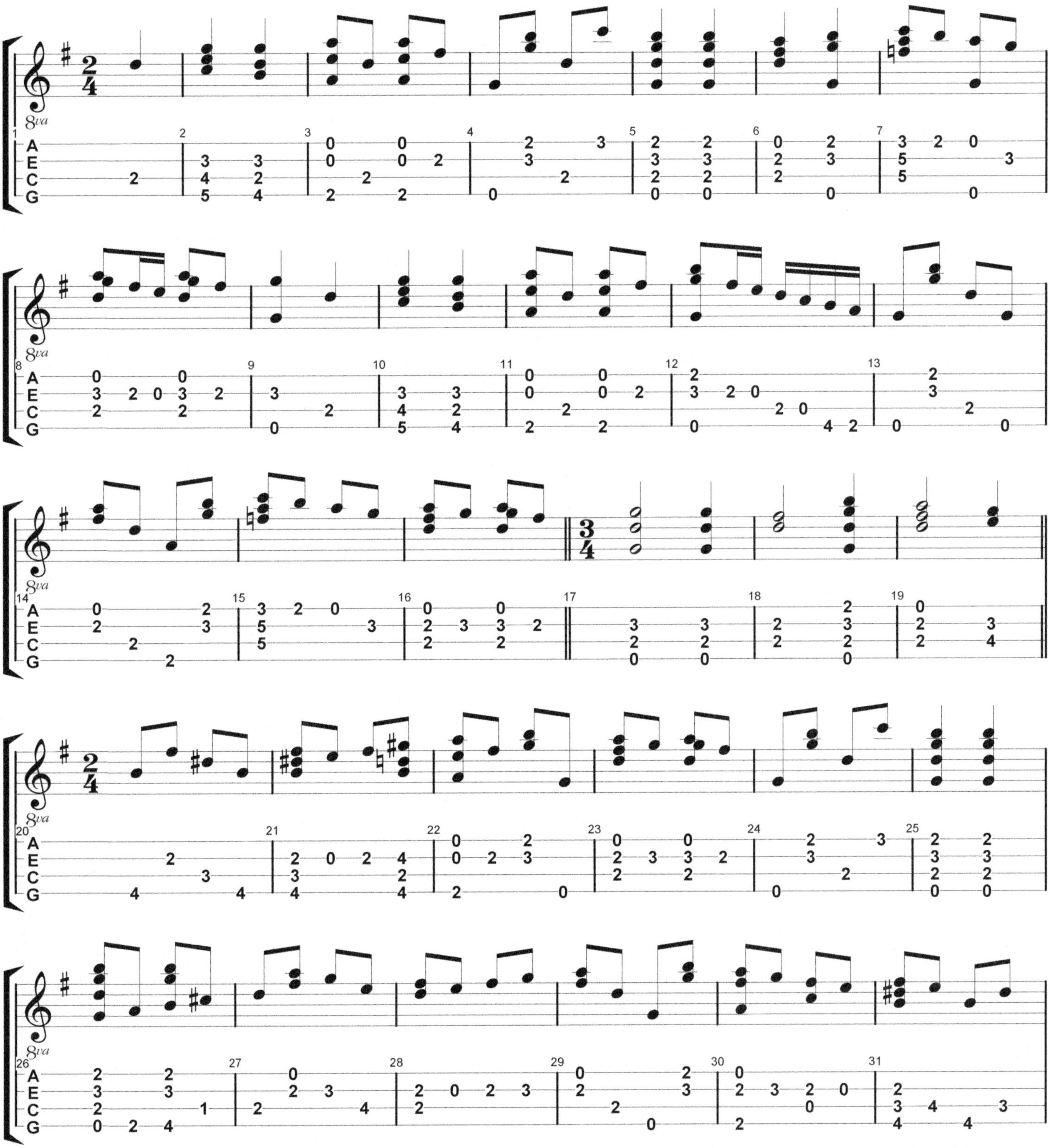

8va
A
E
C
G

Amour ha pouuoir sur les dieus

Jacob Arcadet 1505 -1568

Tablature by Michael Walker

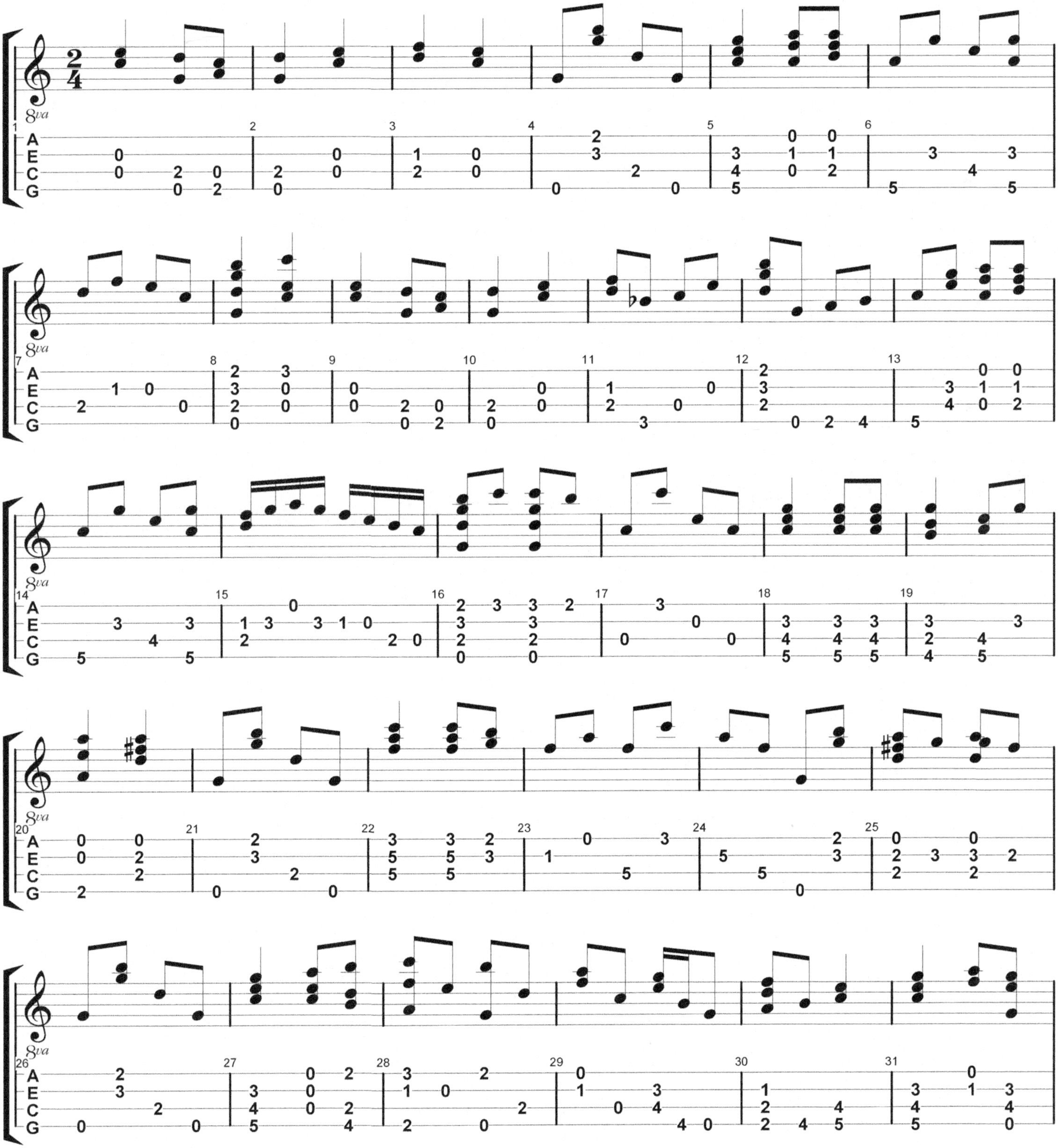

8va
32
A
E
C
G
33
34
35
36
37
38
39
40
41
42
43
44
45

Qui pourra dire la douleur

Jacob Arcadet 1505 - 1568

Tablature by Michael Walker

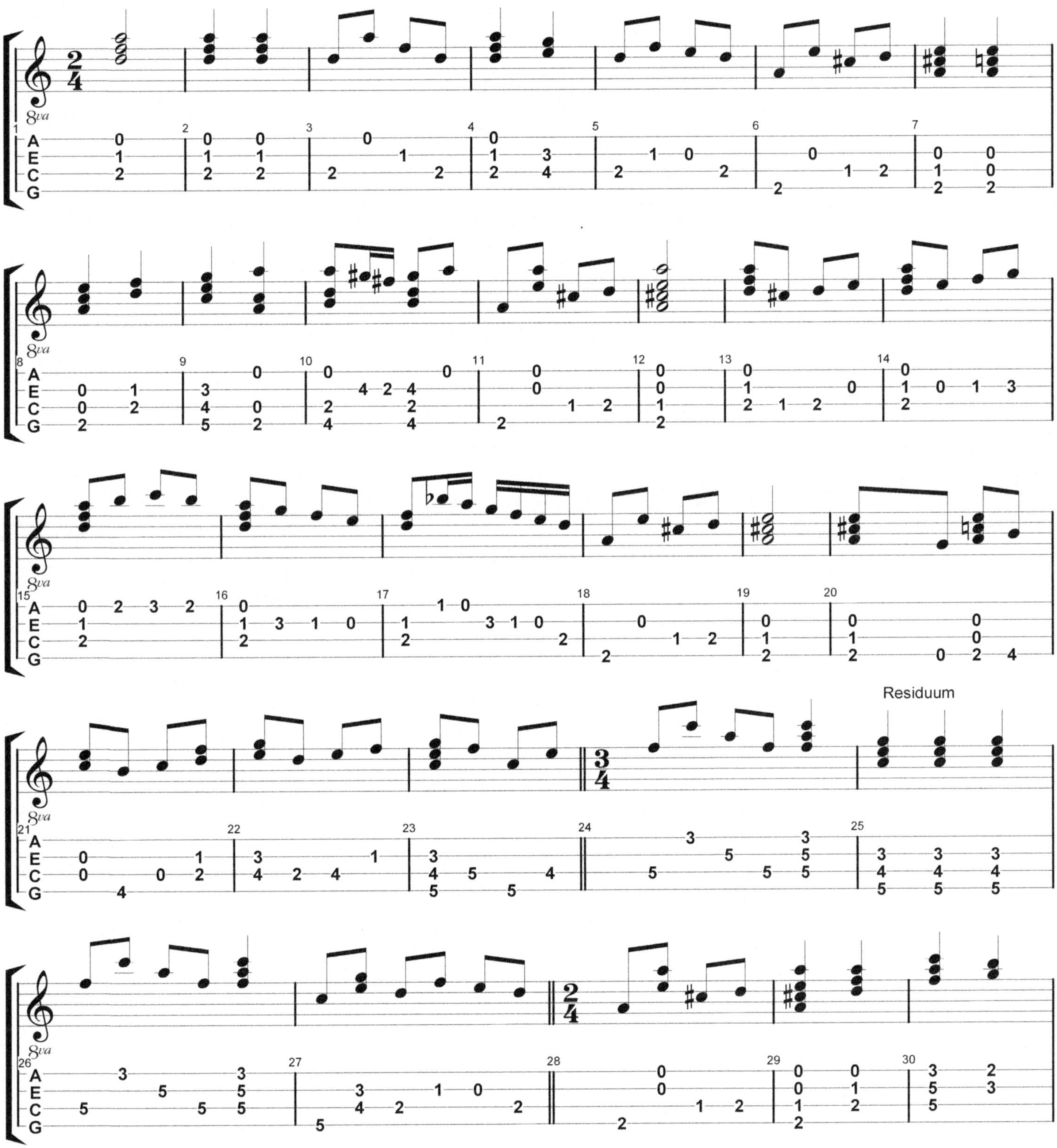

8va
A
E
C
G
31 32 33 34 35
36 37 38 39 40
41 42 43 44 45

Si ce n'est amour qu'est-ce

Jacob Arcadet 1505 - 1568

Tablature by Michael Walker

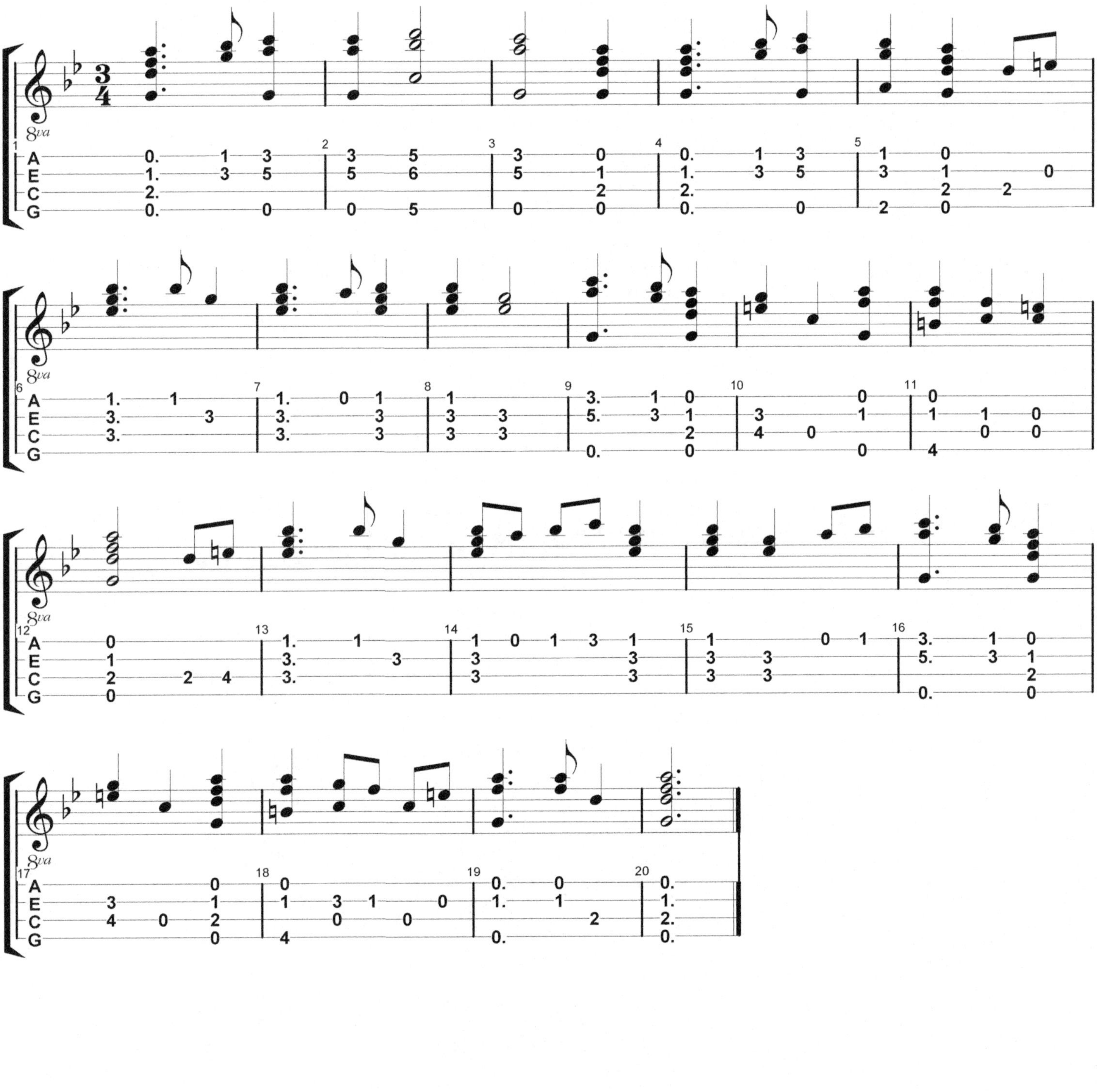

Si j'aime ou non

Adrian Le Roy - 1520 - 1598

Tablature by Michael Walker

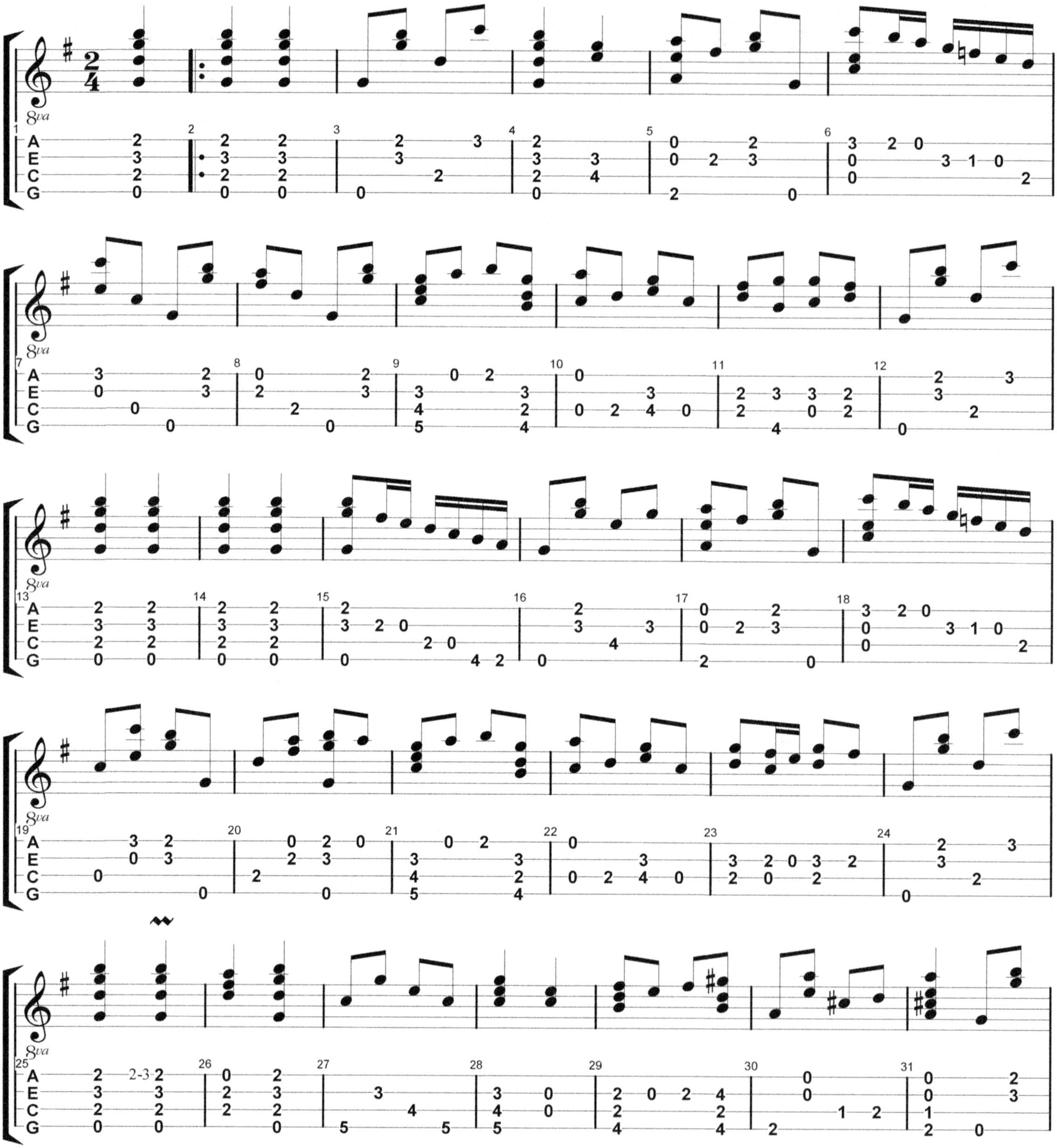

Si j'aime ou non - Adrian Le Roy - 1520 - 1598

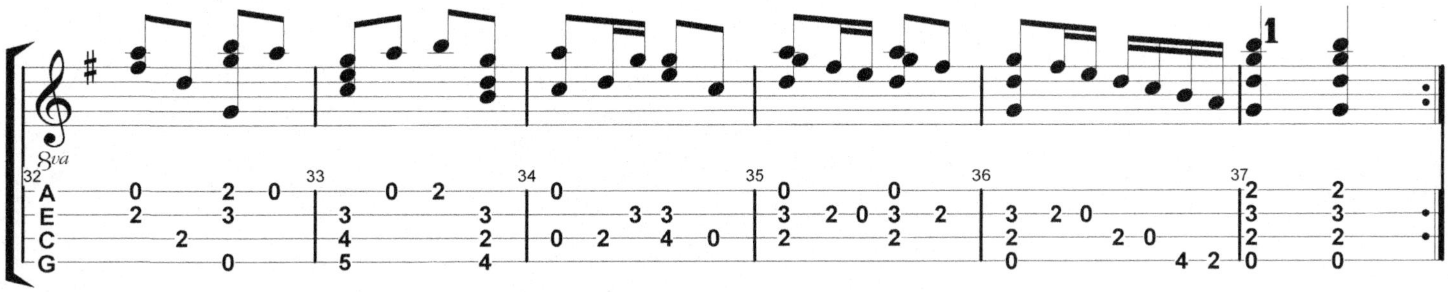

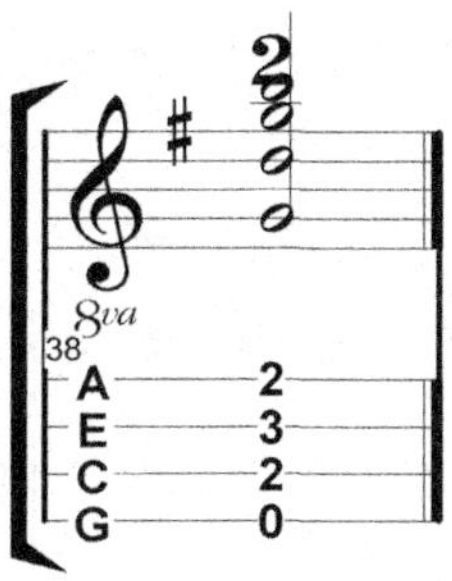

Nous voyons que les hommes

Jacob Arcadet 1505 - 1568

Tablature by Michael Walker

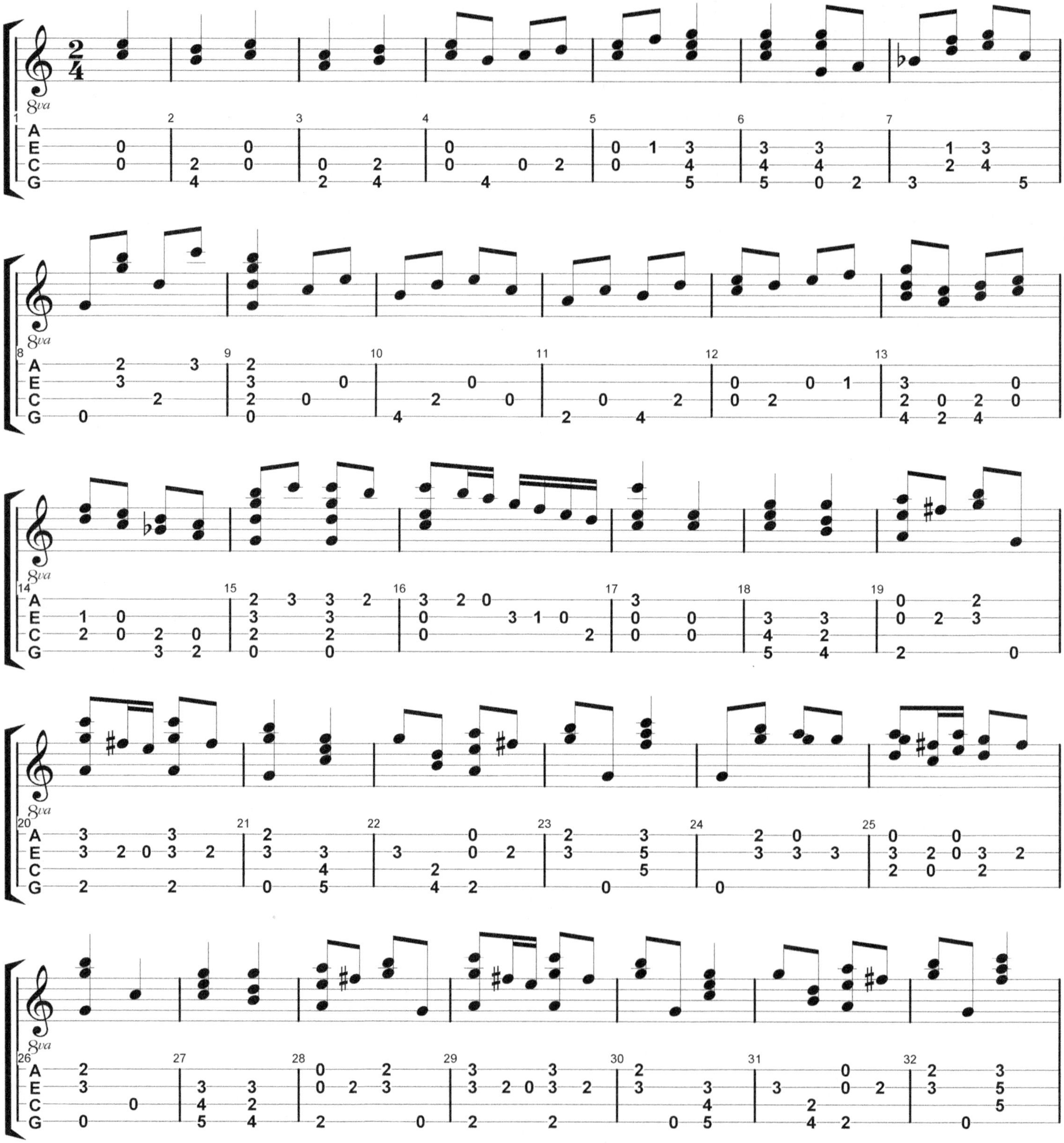

Nous voyons que les hommes - Jacob Arcadet 1505 - 1568

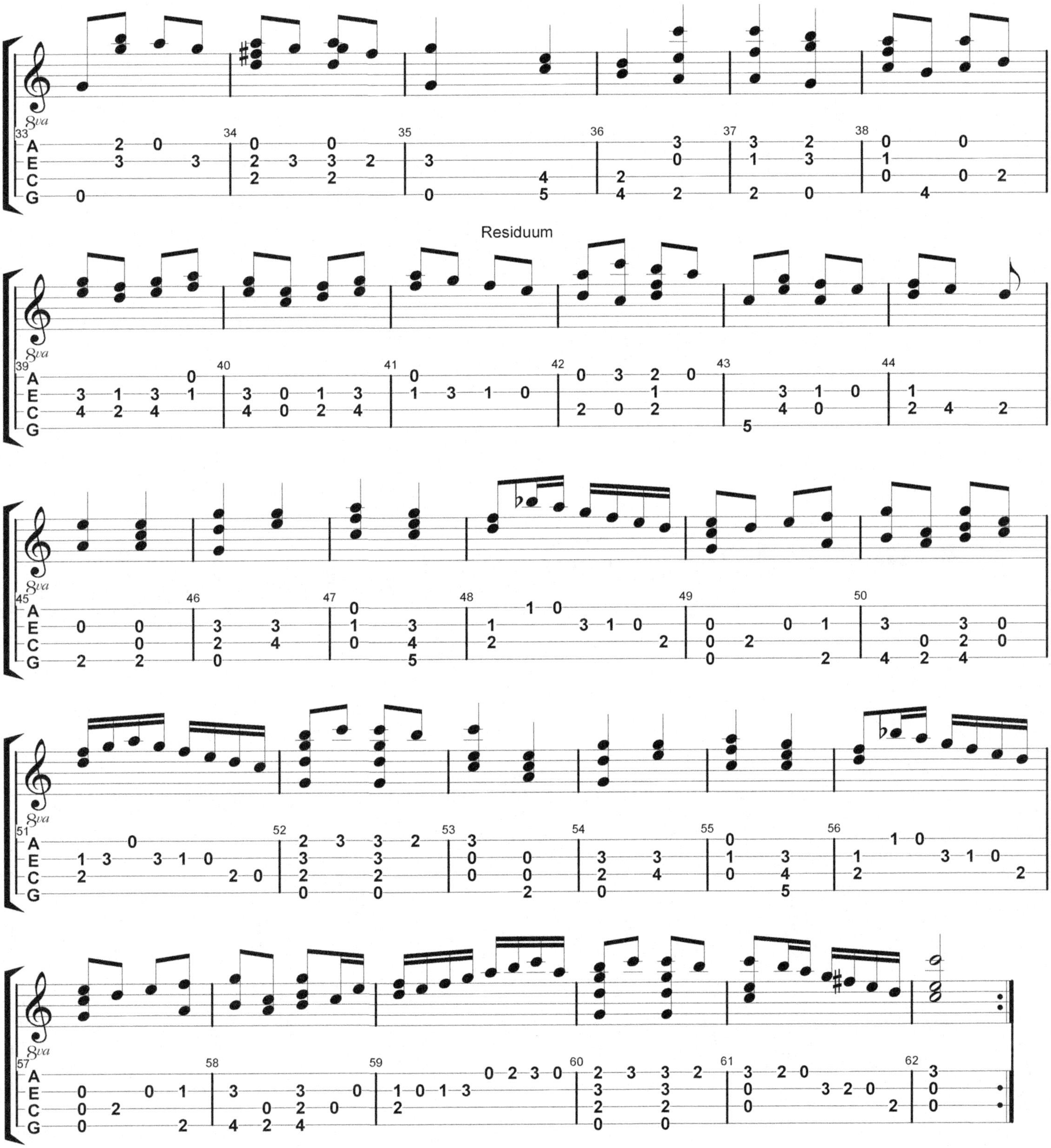

La pastorella mia

Jacob Arcadet 1505 - 1568

Tablature by Michael Walker

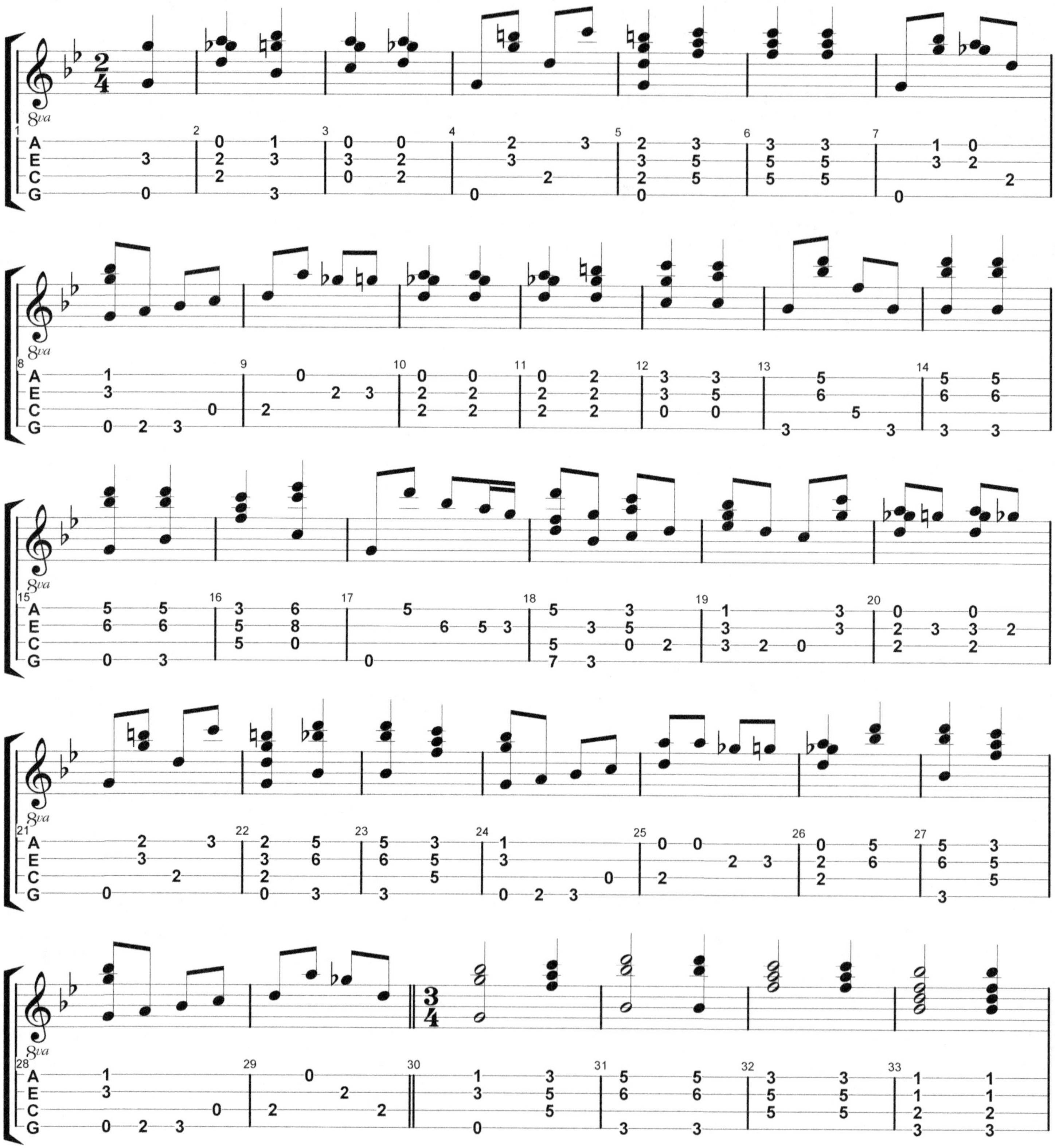

8va
A
E
C
G

Margot labourez les vignes

Jacob Arcadet 1505 - 1568

Tablature by Michael Walker

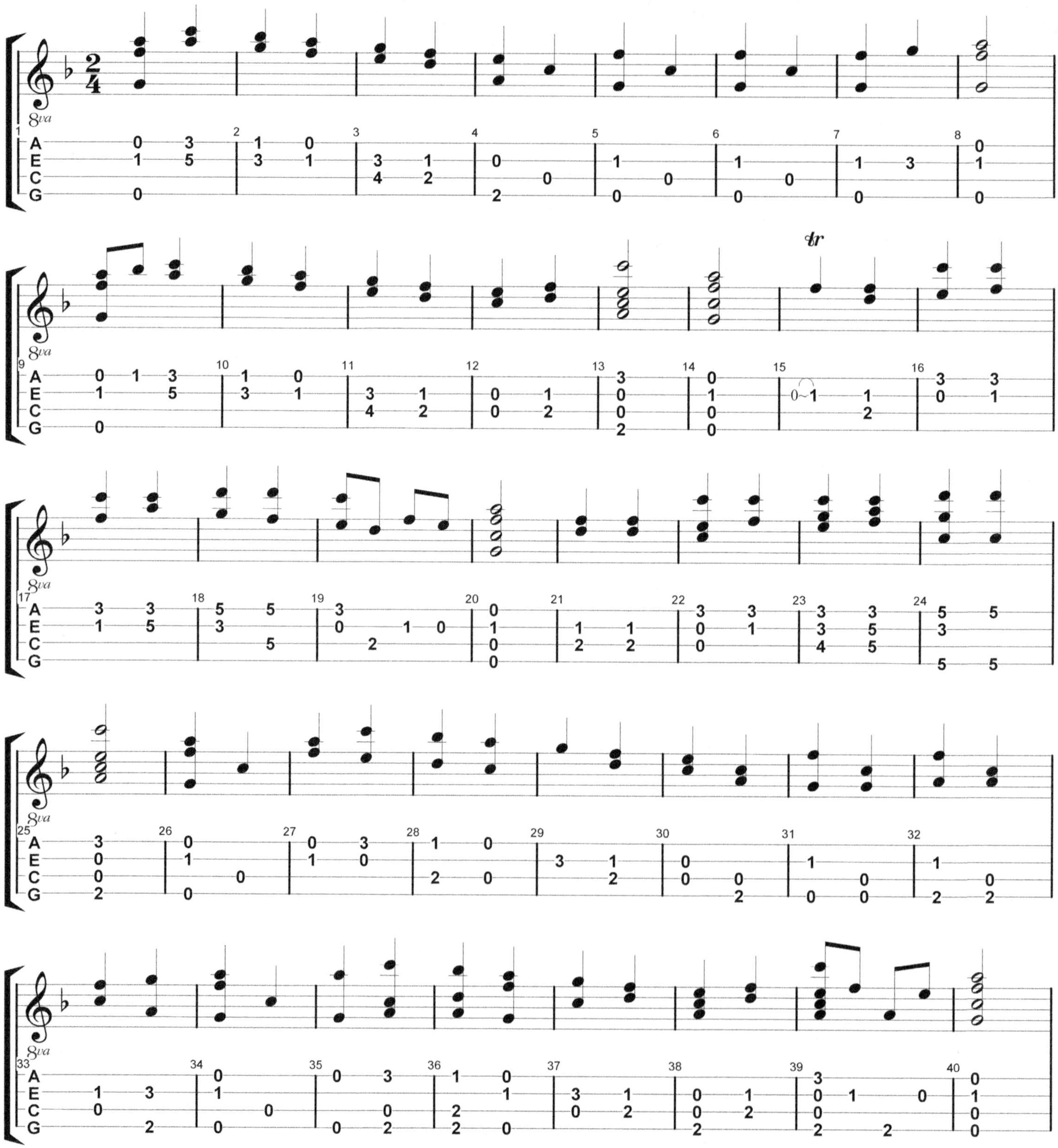

Margot labourez les vignes - Jacob Arcadet 1505 - 1568

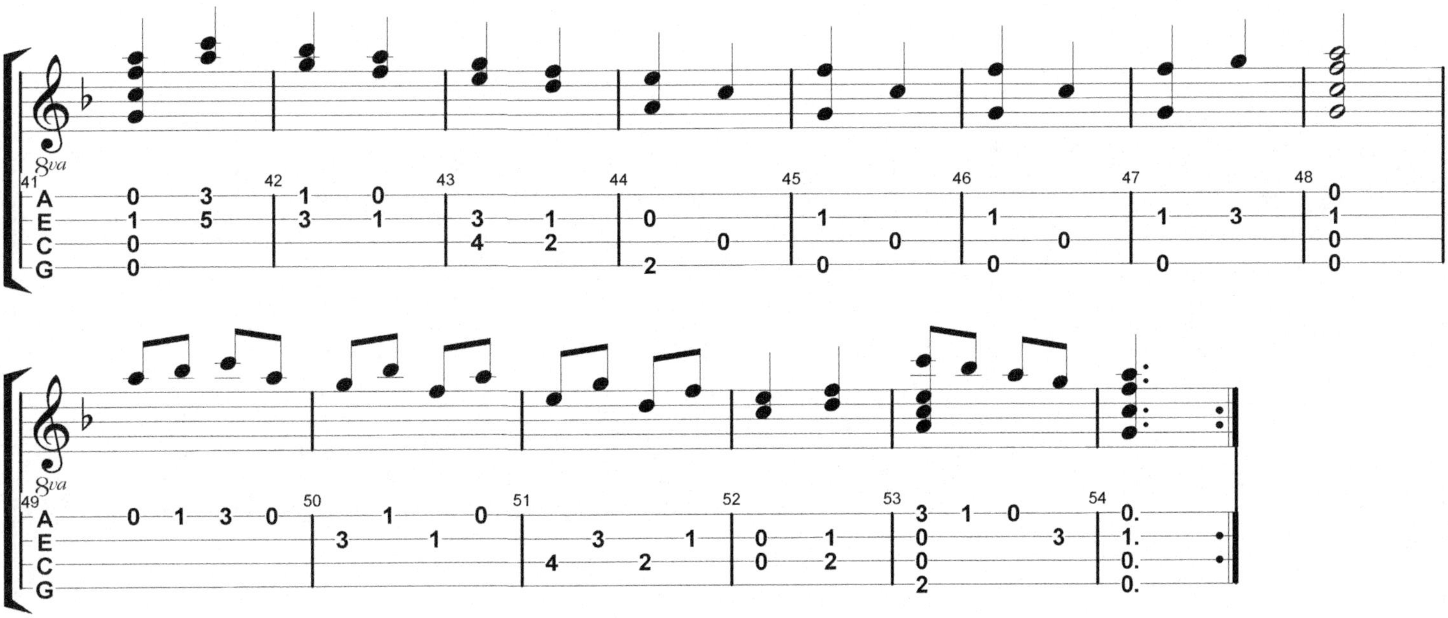

Jamais femme ne sera

Pierre Certon - d. 1572

Tablature by Michael Walker

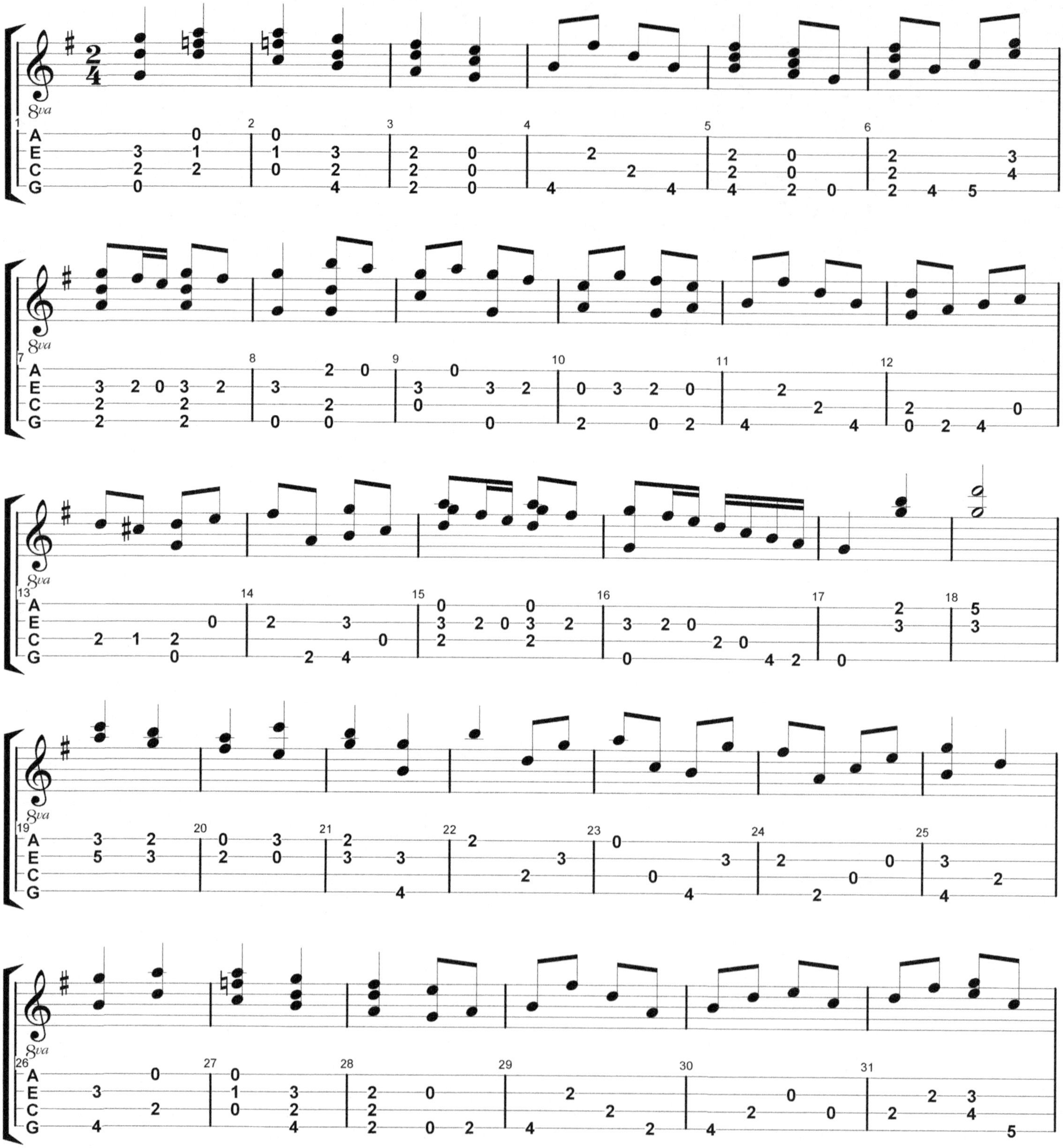

8va
A
E
C
G
8va
A
E
C
G

Amour me sçauriez vous aprendre

Jacob Arcadet 1505 - 1568

Tablature by Michael Walker

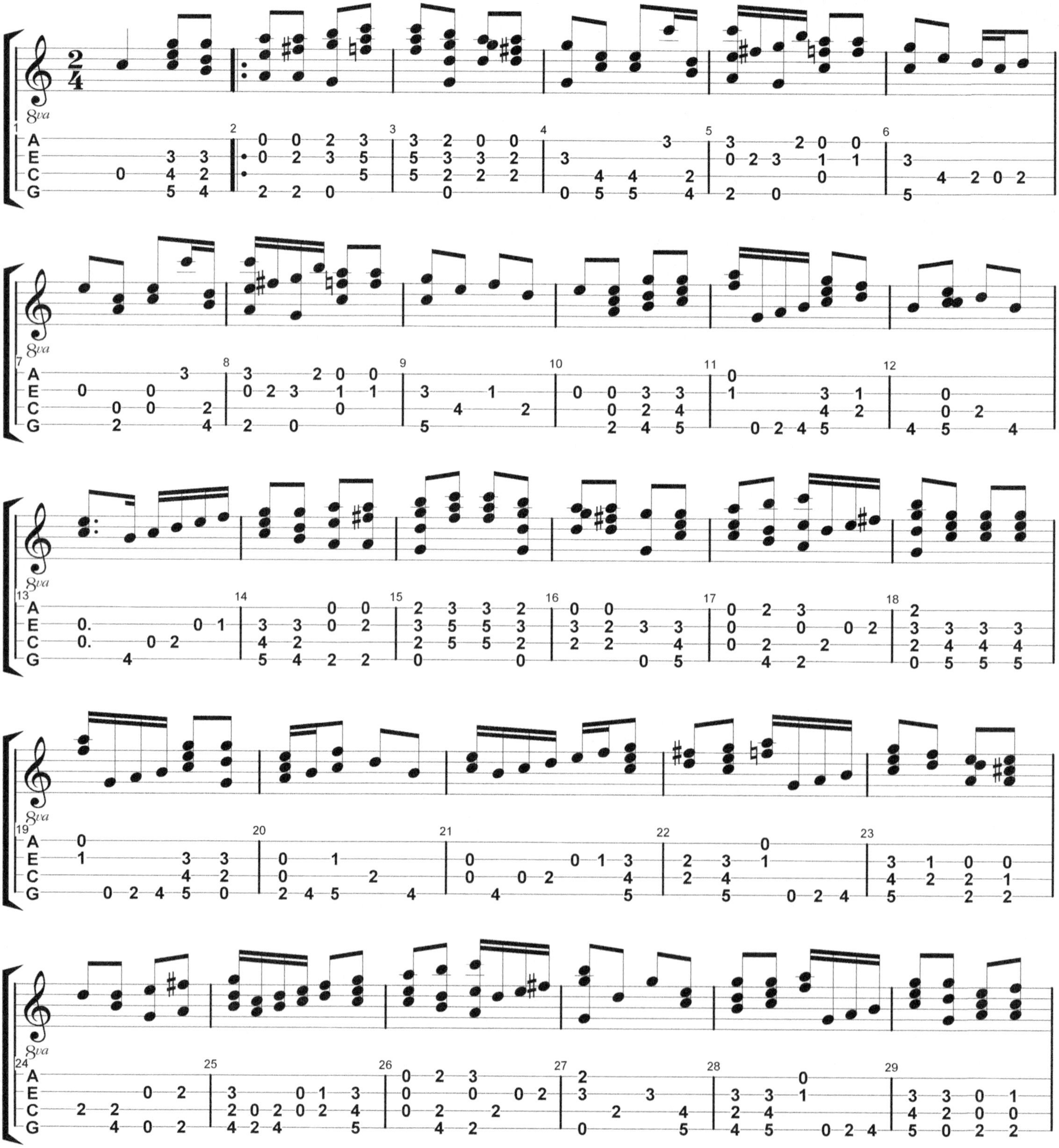

Amour me sçauriez vous aprendre - Jacob Arcadet 1505 - 1568

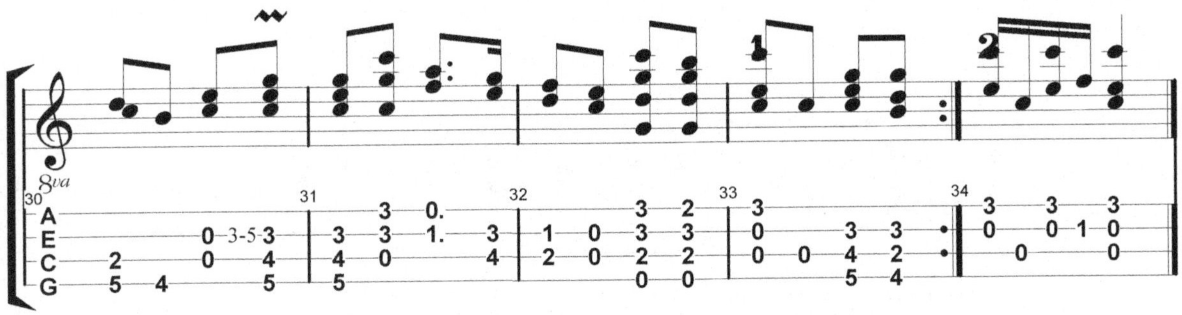

Je sonne la retraitte

Pierre Certon - d. 1572

Tablature by Michael Walker

Je sonne la retraitte - Pierre Certon - d. 1572

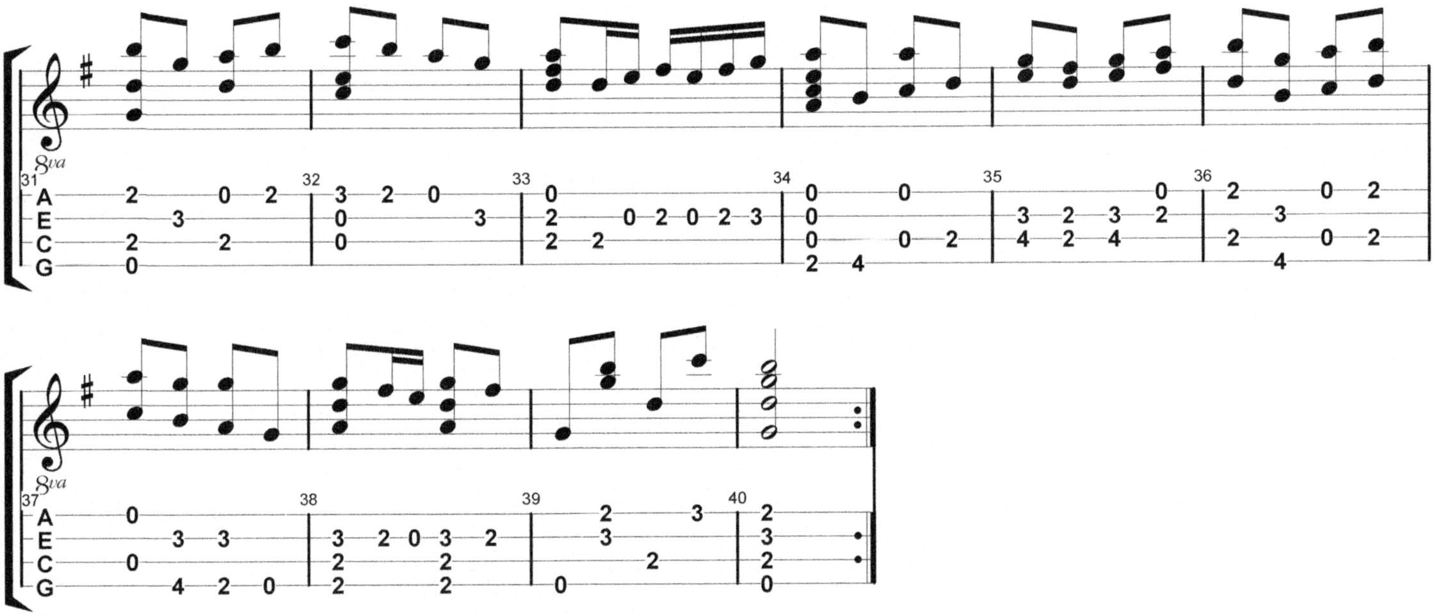

Printed in Great Britain
by Amazon

37246079R00026